A ROMAN SOLDIER'S HANDBOOK

Alison Hawes

Crabtree Publishing Company
www.crabtreebooks.com

Warning! Children should not attempt to make or eat the garum recipe on page 19.

Author: Alison Hawes
Editor: Crystal Sikkens
Project coordinator: Kathy Middleton
Production coordinator: Ken Wright
Prepress technician: Margaret Amy Salter
Series consultant: Gill Matthews

Every effort has been made to trace copyright holders and to obtain their permission for use of copyright material. The authors and publishers would be pleased to rectify any error or omission in future editions. All the Internet addresses given in this book were correct at the time of going to press. The author and publishers regret any inconvenience caused if addresses have changed or sites have ceased to exist, but can accept no responsibility for any such changes.

Picture credits:
Corbis: Colin Dixon/Arcaid 15t
Dreamstime: Peter Szucs 15b,
 Ermine Street Guard Re-enactment Society 4, 5b, 8, 10, 20b
Istockphoto: (Cover) Standby; Thomas Pullicino 11t, Tomboy2290 19b
Shutterstock: (Cover) Mikhail Pogosov, Sue C Matthew Collingwood 21t, Will Iredale 12, Javarman 19t, Verity Johnson 6, 7t, 7b, Lagui 20t, William Attard McCarthy 16, 17, Stephen Mulcahey 9t, Regien Paassen 11b, Rolandino 5t, James Steidl 9b, Sue C 13, Matka Waristka 18, Pippa West 14

Library and Archives Canada Cataloguing in Publication

Hawes, Alison, 1952-
  A Roman soldier's handbook / Alison Hawes.

(Crabtree connections)
Includes index.
ISBN 978-0-7787-9952-8 (bound).--ISBN 978-0-7787-9974-0 (pbk.)

  1. Soldiers--Rome--Juvenile literature. 2. Rome--Army-- Juvenile literature. 3. Rome--History, Military--30 B.C.-- Juvenile literature. I. Title. II. Series: Crabtree connections.

U35.H39 2010   j355.00937   C2010-901511-8

Library of Congress Cataloging-in-Publication Data

Hawes, Alison, 1952-
  A Roman soldier's handbook / Alison Hawes.
    p. cm. -- (Crabtree connections)
  Includes index.
  ISBN 978-0-7787-9952-8 (reinforced lib. bdg. : alk. paper)
  -- ISBN 978-0-7787-9974-0 (pbk. : alk. paper)
  1. Soldiers--Rome--Juvenile literature. 2. Rome--Army--Juvenile literature. 3. Rome--History, Military--30 B.C.-476 A.D.--Juvenile literature. I. Title. II. Series.

  U35.H39 2010
  355.00937--dc22

                                        2010008057

Crabtree Publishing Company
www.crabtreebooks.com   1-800-387-7650
Copyright © 2011 **CRABTREE PUBLISHING COMPANY.** All rights reserved. No part of this publication may be reproduced, stored in a retrieval system or be transmitted in any form or by any means, electronic, mechanical, photocopying, recording, or otherwise, without the prior written permission of Crabtree Publishing Company. Published in the United Kingdom in 2009 by A & C Black Publishers Ltd. The right of the author of this work has been asserted.

Printed in the U.S.A./062010/WO20100815

Published in Canada
Crabtree Publishing
616 Welland Ave.
St. Catharines, Ontario
L2M 5V6

Published in the United States
Crabtree Publishing
PMB 59051
350 Fifth Avenue, 59th Floor
New York, New York 10118

CONTENTS

1: SO YOU WANT TO BE A ROMAN SOLDIER?

Life as a Roman **soldier** is not easy. It is a hard, dangerous job. Only the strongest and fittest people can join the army.

WANT TO JOIN?

The good news is that being in the army means you will be:
- well fed
- well paid
- well traveled
- well looked after when you **retire**

Do you want to be a Roman soldier? If so, you must answer yes to all these questions:

1. Are you about 18 years old? ☐
2. Are you unmarried? ☐
3. Are you a citizen of the **Roman Empire**? ☐
4. Are you willing to obey orders without question? ☐

If you join, you must stay in the army for 25 years!

You must have good eyesight. In battle, you will need to see any signals that are given.

You must have good hearing. In battle, you will need to hear your orders.

You need to be strong. You will have a lot of gear to carry.

You need to be fit. There will be a lot of marching.

SPEAKING THE LANGUAGE

If you don't speak **Latin** (perhaps you are from France or Spain), you must learn it.

All your training and orders will be given in Latin.

Intente! (Attention!)

TOP TIP

If you know someone important, ask them to write a letter of recommendation for you. This will help you get into the army.

5

2: THE UNIFORM

Your basic uniform consists of a knee-length **tunic** with short sleeves and a pair of open leather boots.

WINTER WEAR

In winter, you will wear a long-sleeved tunic, pants, socks, and closed boots. You will also be given a woolen cloak to keep you warm.

HELMET

Your helmet will be made of brass or iron. Pieces on the side stick out and protect your face. Pieces on the back stick out and protect your neck.

Tie your helmet under the chin using the leather strap.

Leather strap

BODY ARMOR

Roman soldiers wear three different types of body armor:

Ring-mail armor: A ring-mail shirt is very heavy. Most Roman soldiers wear this type of armor.

Fish-scale armor: Fish-scale armor is made up of tiny pieces of metal sewn onto leather. **Officers** usually wear this type of armor.

Plate armor: Plate armor is made up of thin, overlapping bands of metal. Both regular soldiers and officers wear this type of armor.

Your shirt will be made of hundreds of linked metal rings.

A short-sleeved metal jacket is held together with hooks, laces, and straps.

TOP TIP

Remember to wear a scarf under your armor. It will stop the metal from digging into your neck!

You can use five weapons: a sword, a shield, a dagger, and two throwing spears.

YOUR SWORD

The sword (gladius) is light and about 20 inches (51 cm) long. It has a sharp, iron blade. It makes a good stabbing weapon. You wear it on the right side of your body at your waist.

USING YOUR WEAPONS

- Use your sword in your right hand (even if you are left-handed). You can then stand in close formation, ready to march into battle.
- Your dagger (pugio) is even smaller than your sword. If you lose your sword in battle, use your dagger instead.
- Your shield (scutum) is curved and rectangular so it fits around your body to protect it. It deflects most blows.

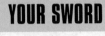
A sword

Several layers of wood are glued together to make your shield strong but light.

Boss

- In battle, use your shield as a weapon. Smash the metal boss into your enemy and then stab at him with your sword.
- At the start of battle, throw your spear (pilum) at the enemy. The metal tip of the 6.5-foot (2 m) long pilum is so sharp it can pierce metal body armor.
- If a spear misses the enemy and hits the ground, it will fall apart. This means your enemy cannot throw it back at you.

Throwing a spear

9

4: TRAINING

You will go to training camp when you first join the army. Here, you will spend most of your time keeping fit and learning how to use your weapons.

Basic training lasts for about four months.

KEEPING FIT

Most days you will be running, marching, swimming, or wrestling.

WEAPONS TRAINING

You start your training with wooden weapons and move on to the real thing when you are skilled enough.

LONG MARCHES

Every ten days, you will go on a long march. You will march about 20 miles (32 km) each time, in full uniform and carrying your weapons and kit.

MAKING CAMP

You will share a goatskin tent with seven other soldiers. You must set up camp quickly. All camps are made the same way:
- dig a ditch
- put up a fence
- put up the tents

SIGNALS

You will be taught to recognize and obey signals given in battle. Some signals are given on a horn or trumpet. Others are given with banners called **standards**.

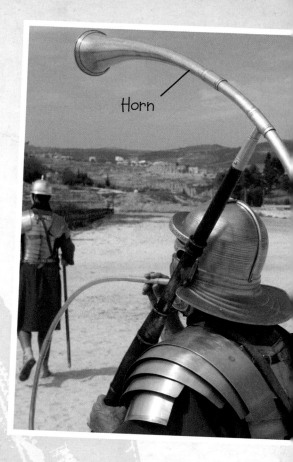

Horn

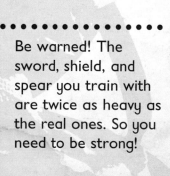

Be warned! The sword, shield, and spear you train with are twice as heavy as the real ones. So you need to be strong!

5. FIGHTING BATTLES

Once you have mastered how to use your weapons, you must then learn how to fight successfully in a battle.

BATTLE FORMATION

When you march into battle you must not march or run ahead on your own. You march into battle in **formation**. Roman soldiers win battles because they fight together as one **unit**.

FIGHTING MACHINES

When you are attacking a **fort**, you will have to build fighting machines to help you.

This machine is called an onager. Use it to hurl big rocks or piles of stones at your enemy.

THE TORTOISE

If you need to get up close to an enemy fort, get into the tortoise formation with the soldiers next to you for protection.

The shields protect you from arrows and rocks thrown from above.

SHEDS AND TOWERS

If you need to break into a fort, you must build special sheds and towers to help you.

6. BUILDING PROJECTS

It's hard work being a Roman soldier. When you are not training or fighting, you will be given a lot of building work to do.

ROAD BUILDERS

A lot of your time will be spent building roads and bridges. Soldiers can move from place to place quickly on good roads and bridges.

Good roads mean letters from home will arrive sooner.

Road building is hard work. Build them fast, but build them to last.

TOP TIP

It helps to have a special skill, such as being good at writing or looking after horses. Then you won't have to do the boring jobs, such as guard duty or cleaning.

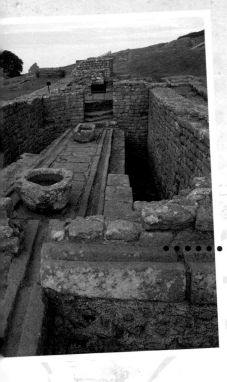

FORTS

You may also have to build a fort to live in. Most forts are built of wood, but you may have to help rebuild one in stone. That will make it stronger and last longer. At a fort, you will sleep in a room rather than a tent. You will share it with the other soldiers in your unit.

Life in a fort is better than life on the road. Each fort has its own baths, hospital, toilets, and bakery.

TOWNS

Towns are often built up around forts. You could be asked to help lay out the streets, dig a well, or build an **aqueduct** or the town walls.

Aqueducts bring fresh, clean water from the hills to the town.

15

7: REWARDS AND PUNISHMENTS

Soldiers who win battles or save lives will be rewarded. You could be given money or a special medal or crown to wear. Most of the rewards go to the officers, not the regular soldiers.

HOW TO BECOME A CENTURION

A regular soldier like you can become a **centurion** if you are:
- brave
- smart
- and if you work hard

Officers wear golden crowns and medals when they are on **parade**.

As an officer, you will be paid much more than regular soldiers. You will wear a crest on your helmet and leg guards, so everyone knows that you are an officer.

PUNISHMENTS

Obey orders and work hard at all times. The officers will punish you if you don't. If you are lazy, an officer might:

- hit you with his cane
- cut your food **rations**
- give you more work to do

But for something more serious, such as stealing, you could be beaten.

Centurions wear their swords and daggers on the opposite side to regular soldiers.

Cane

8. WHAT YOU WILL EAT

Roman soldiers eat well. Good food will keep you strong and healthy. What you eat depends on whether you are on the march or in a fort.

ON THE MARCH

Soldiers on the move eat dried, salted, or smoked foods. Hard biscuits, bacon, cheese, and wine will keep for a few days without going bad.

IN A FORT

You will eat a wider range of food in a fort. Forts house animals for fresh meat, and there will be fresh vegetables to eat. You will also get the chance to hunt for food.

You may be able to hunt birds or deer or catch fish and shellfish. It depends on where your camp is.

Your daily food ration will include:
- bread
- olive oil
- meat
- wine

You need to eat a lot of bread (panis). It gives you energy. Each group of soldiers has two stones to grind wheat into flour to make bread.

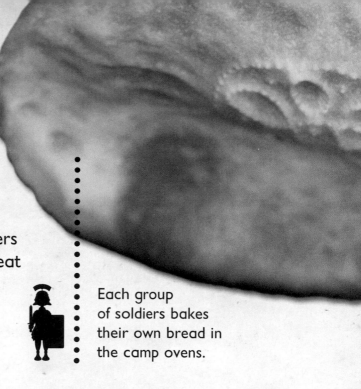

Each group of soldiers bakes their own bread in the camp ovens.

FISH SAUCE (GARUM)

Most soldiers keep a small flask of garum in their kit. You can add this salty, fishy sauce to almost everything you eat.

Garum recipe for soldiers

You will need:
Dried herbs
Fatty fish (anchovies or sardines)
Salt
Cooking pot with a lid

1. Put a thin layer of herbs in the pot.
2. Top with a layer of fish.
3. Cover with a thick layer of salt.
4. Add more layers until the pot is full.
5. Leave the pot in a hot, sunny place.
6. Stir the mixture every day.
7. In a month, the garum should be runny and very smelly. Delicious!

9: WHAT YOU WILL GET PAID

You get some money when you first join the army. After that you will earn about 300 **denarii** a year. You might get extra pay when you win a battle or when Rome gets a new **emperor**.

A silver denarius

SOLDIER'S EXPENSES

Most of your pay will go toward food, bedding, and your uniform.

Look after your weapons. You will have to buy new ones if you don't!

———— Sword

SPARE CASH

You will have a bit of spare cash when you have paid for all your expenses. You can use that money for fun!

Use some of your hard-earned money to spend an afternoon at the baths with your friends.

TOP TIP

Don't spend all your spare cash. You will need to save for retirement.

RETIREMENT

You will be given about ten years' pay when you retire. You will also get your savings from the savings fund.

DEATH

Your burial fund will pay for your funeral when you die.

GLOSSARY

aqueduct A stone structure that channels water from its source to a town

centurion An officer in the Roman army

denarii Roman coins

emperor The ruler of an empire

formation An arrangement of troops in a line, column, or other order

fort A well-defended place where soldiers live

Latin The language spoken by the Romans

officers The people in charge of the regular soldiers

parade A formation of a body of troops before an officer of higher rank

ration A set amount of food given to a soldier in one day

retire To stop doing paid work

Roman Empire All the countries and land occupied by the Romans

soldier There were two kinds of Roman soldiers—legionaries and auxiliaries. This book tells you about legionary soldiers from the first century AD

standards The special banners carried by the Roman armies

tunic A long, loose piece of clothing usually knee-length or longer

unit A group

FURTHER INFORMATION

WEB SITES

Find out about the Roman army at the Web site of the British Broadcasting Corporation (BBC): **www.bbc.co.uk/schools/romans/army.shtml**

Learn about some of the incredible Roman constructions at: **www.roman-empire.net/children/builders.html**

BOOKS

Gladiators and Roman Soldiers (Fierce Fighters) by Charlotte Guillain. Raintree (2010)

How to be a Roman Soldier by Fiona MacDonald. National Geographic Children's Books (2008)

Romans: Dress, Eat, Write and Play just like the Romans (Hands-On History) by Fiona Macdonald. Crabtree Publishing Company (2008)

Life in Ancient Rome (Peoples of the Ancient World) by Shilpa Mehta-Jones. Crabtree Publishing Company (2005)

INDEX

J
937
H

HAWES, ALISON

A ROMAN SOLDIER'S
HANDBOOK

DATE			

BAKER & TAYLOR